the tide will take it

the tide will take it

Georgina Woods

*It is because of the joy in my heart
that I am your fit mourner.*

Judith Wright, 'Letter to a Friend'

PUNCHER & WATTMANN

First published in 2021
Published by Puncher and Wattmann
PO Box 279
Waratah NSW 2298

https://www.puncherandwattmann.com
web@puncherandwattmann.com

ISBN   9781922571304

Cover design by Miranda Douglas
Typesetting by Morgan Arnett
Printed by Lightning Source International

NATIONAL LIBRARY OF AUSTRALIA
A catalogue record for this book is available from the National Library of Australia

Australian Government | Australia Council for the Arts

This project has been assisted by the Australian Government through the Australia Council, its arts funding and advisory body.

Contents

Acknowledgement of Country

i

Water descends to Awabakal country
over weeks from Gringai, Darkinjung,
Gamilaraay and Wiradjuri country,
through Wonnarua and Worimi country.
As it comes it lifts; it rests;
it brings; it parts.

ii

Embroidered moss-spring
on montane swampland
draws water from night
and lays it loving down at dawn
in beads growing heavy
joining and running.

In western basalt gullies
memory lights in clouds
of plum-heads and finches.
A gun's retort echoes and the flock
scatters in alarm and cuts
transmission.

From Yengo's sandstone cliffs
rain carves animal shapes,
erodes and carries them leaking
down the Wollombi. Minerals
drop out and come to rest
in sediment.

iii

When the names are wrong
the story runs off over land
beaten under hoof and drags
the soil with it.

Decades-slow water presses up
from layered Permian pages.
Stories of warm Gondwana
and diluvian times.
They're ripped up now
and burned like the banned,
as tides again rise.

What we touch we beat hard or drown.
Fast, too fast, the stream runs.
The poor old river cuts deep
between its high clenched banks
nursing chains of pools
and bull-oak forest remnants.

iv

At the estuary, muscly rills
on the river's back
haul ropes of current
arm over arm
trailing banderole
in wind-woven ribbons.

There is grief in the pull
sobbing and depositing silt

over weeks and centuries
'round these mangroves.

There are not words for the curls
confusing 'round Ash Island
where river meets tide
and an old land contends
with the currents.

Water song

At dusk the limpid blue
and scent of cold water
call you out
into indigo, sweep you
down to the sand spit,
where you scatter
the avocets.

Mullet hang in the current,
nuzzling the beloved
tide. If you harbour
any knot of self, let it
be combed and stroked
from you by the ebb
as detritus.

The tide will take it.
There is that comfort:
what you discard in shame
the sea will draw away.
Silver gulls pick off
the mess blown out
the heads by westerlies.

Beyond the breakwall,
a rolling swell arches
her back and spreads like
an elephantine
siren. Beneath it,
the depth lows
and is answered

with a song, to
king tide, who comes
for our bulwarks, leaving
sand on the doorstep.
Hold fast, cries the
seawall, but there's
no need for that.
Just take it.

Keeping records

Rail lines curled as fire swept
over the Junee grassland.
Senator Heffernan eyed his paddock
of roasted mutton in January 2006—
the hottest day,
of the hottest year
of the hottest decade.

"It was a bugger of a day, mate."

Superlatives fail like budgies in this heat,
heaped in fading piles of old news.

How hot *is* the hottest?
It was summer 2009,
when flying foxes fell
and the road melted
and we ran with our kids
into January 2013:
the hottest year, summer, month and day
            on record...

... but not for long.

Blossoms are perplexed and have poor timing.
They rush out in the winter warmth like pre-school ballerinas
jumping stage cues in sweet tulle dresses
wandering confused on dark stages,
hushed and shrivelled away by a frosty
dance mistress, tapping...

plink, plink, plink, the dripping
cryosphere frets Pacific babies through the night.
Their mothers soothe them with mango pulp
the colour of dry suits worn by scientists
grimly stumping across white-blue ice-sheet.
They record the heat
and melt
and eat
spam lunches,
                            waiting out the

winds rushing up to Newcastle where
coal carriers loom beside our tinny,
remorseless as jelly fish, bumping
eyelessly past—
            when the ice is gone,
                        and our houses sunk,
Global Triumph will still be gliding over us.

Run it aground, *Aurora Low-low.*
Send it after *Pasha Bulker*
surfing onto sand like a starved shearwater
or a million-dollar Collaroy beach pad
making double page wow for about an hour
while thirty million Bangladeshis brace
against the tide.

Ten years feel like a century:
here we crouch again
under a wheeling gyre,
one in one hundred
times
a year

ten years
after we went
to Copenhagen
and learned the koans
of climate politics—
Pam roaring with 80kn winds through
Vanuatu's fringe of foliage.
The negotiations are category five as Haiyan's eye
fixes on Tacloban and

The beauty of the world
         the paragon of animals

hides under mattresses
under banging roof tin:

      fee   *fi*   *fo*   *fum*

coming for us, ripping the lids
off rickety sheds.

      "…never seen anything like it…"

says no one

after a few more years
of thunder giants
like Yasi, Haiyan and Pam.

We reap in floods the miracles we've sown:
Pakistan surrenders under Indus.
Cam Pha succumbs to poisonous slurry spilling
from flooded coal mines and the first falls in years

dampen hay in Queensland and fill the air with wine-
scent bubbling up through drains in Miami Beach—
so shopkeepers wear plastic bags on their boots.
Land prices and shopping malls rise with the tides.
Proud owners wad money up and stuff it
under the door jamb,
        casting looks
            to the sea:
                "Mayhem is coming."

So the great wet breaks loose,
and reclaims its domain.

Floodwater hangs heavy above you,
your nieces and nephews.
Harken to muffled sirens
and broken crystal.

It creeps high—engulfing us in angry blue,
the deep part of the bruise.

In that colour we will recall
in that light, our abulia,
in that silence, our fealty,
to each other,
and the waters
that have carried us.

[Notes]

"It was a bugger of a day" Senator Bill Heffernan, quoted in Daniel Lewis,
   3 January 2006. 'Fire victims count the cost,' *Sydney Morning Herald*.
Heat records drawn from Bureau of Meteorology *Special Climate Statements*
   2 March 2007, 20 March 2008, 4 February 2009, 8 February 2011, 7 January 2013,
   15 March 2013.
"The beauty of the world! The paragon of animals!" Shakespeare. *Hamlet*.
   Act II Sc. ii.
"…never seen anything like it" BOM forecaster Terry Ryan, quoted in Peter
   Munro and Mark Russell, 6 February 2011. 'Victoria swamped: storm wreaks
   havoc,' *The Age*.
"Mayhem is coming" Philip Stoddard, Mayor of South Miami, quoted in Robin
   McKee 11 July 2014. 'Miami, the great world city, is drowning while the powers
   that be look away' *The Guardian*. http://www.theguardian.com/world/2014/
   jul/11/miami-drowning-climate-change-deniers-sea-levels-rising

Open the window and let her fly out

Falena you're beating your wings on my ear for escape.
Your hunters are taken in custody. Go now, you
friable moon slave: stop bumping your head on the glass.

Your liberty shivers in silvery gloom with my own and
my young friend whose dad told me, *men are just visual,*
in his relief that she's pretty enough to attract one.

I'm watching them watching themselves being watched as they preen.
Shivering wing-hems, brushing their downy soft
thigh hairs for comfort, or fiddling the clasp of a bracelet.

Falena, the silvery ball that they gave you is not the moon.
Put it away from you. It will enthral you with
mirror-light caught from your ersatz self: shiny and eye-catching.

Its surface is polished with touching but passionless.
Nestled in moth suede it's poised to be grabbed and
put on display with a pin through the abdomen.

Paradise Losing

Le paradis n'est pas artificiel,
but melting and fermenting, it seems.
The panting, perishing white lemuroid
possum can't get enough water,
can't cool her febrile body,
drops from the canopy of a thousand-year old tree,
in a white whoosh of rushing light.

Le paradis n'est pas artificiel,
but unpredictable, these days.
Short-tailed shearwaters cruise southward,
but their fruitless fishing for squid
during this too-hot November,
leaves them knackered, and the shore-break delivers
them to us as they give up the ghost.

Le paradis n'est pas artificiel,
but becoming simpler, no doubt.
The great blue homeland acidifies
and corrodes its little calcite prawns,
absorbs them, with a sigh, into the same soup
that sloshes over the coral beds,
turning them a general algal brown.

[Notes]

"Le paradis n'est pas artificiel" Ezra Pound in *The Pisan Cantos* (Cantos 74, 76, 77
and 83) alluding to Baudelaire's 'Les Paradis Artificiels'

The Tao of birding

i.   golden plovers

I think I won't be seen.
I take slow steps and keep
my arms down.

My boot batters
a pebble that startles
a golden plover.

It paces across the spit.
Now there are half-a-dozen
unhidden birds appearing:

raindrops on sand.
The way that can be seen
is not the shorebird way.

Apparition: baby lapwing Tao masters
in my path, wary like prawns,
relaxed as warming ice.

Be still and time will clear
muddied water. Once you get
your eyes, birds appear.

ii.   superb lyrebird

Furtive at the edge of a dry creek,
a silhouette, dark unfeatured.

The heir of primeval song dashes
for fern cover, flashing a shadow flag.

Drawn low, he turns the ground-drop,
gathering garlands of sound in hollows carved

from the mountain. Take the world into
your throat, open like a valley: swallow

and release any forest song.
Be a riverbed unto others.

iii.   *rufous scrub bird*

We anticipate a rufous scrub bird.
It is here, and so are we, but not yet met.
Like Gautama, we are prepared to wait.
Under a tree: emptying our minds.

Like wisdom it is feral, cryptic.
It prefers to remain so. It bides
in dense understorey. Not furtive, no.
It throws back its head and calls
full-throated behind a curtain of leaves.

[Notes]

"relaxed as warming ice" and "Be still and time will clear the muddied water" are
adapted from various translations of Chapter 15 of the *Tao Te Ching*.

Clarissa

She had stolen flowers herself to crown her
guests with garlands picked from local gardens.
We had come to welcome her eldest child to
womanhood at last.

Greeting us vivaciously, drink in hand, she
dolloped charming malapropism into
ardent conversation like fragrant Cointreau
into her champagne.

Later her third husband took precedence and
made a lengthy toast to the daughter with no
mention of her mother, his wife, who stood
resplendent behind him.

Sweeping on my own the next morning, I
gathered dying blooms into posies and made
a wish with Beatrice that I could eat his
heart in the market.

Sand whiting

A thing dropped
into a clear pool will draw fish
seeking food.

So Dante and Beatrice were received
by ambitious hungry lights
in the second circle of paradise.

And so it is in limpid waves behind
the shore-break at Bar Beach — turquoise, just like
a circle of heaven on holy days
as the sun strikes sheer
through the sea's restless face.

Lucent sand whiting hang unseen
and I am drawn to the light from
their flanks. Mirror-winks
from distant wreck survivors.
My keen heart-jolt flashes back
in answer.

Between breaths
garlanded with streamers
I follow their turn,
salt-blurred among
the weed-manes.

Rites of passage
Hunter Valley, winter 2016

The old man slowed with the cold as his days grew shorter.
His wife prepared pills and propped his head.
He swallowed two mouthfuls of mint tea but did
not speak. The maid arrived as he drew back
with fewer, shorter breaths and left.
The mother arrived to comfort the widow.
                              And so the rites began.

On the first day, the widow lit a candle. The maid
carted discarded household parts. The mother
cut wood for the fire. The doctor came and signed
the first piece of paper. They cleaned and oiled the old
man with oregano and dressed him in a kaftan.
The widow started the gennie at dusk. They carried
him on a sheet to the cold back room.

On the second day, the maid and the mother burned
piles of paper, words in ash collapsed
at the touch. The old man's daughter came,
asking for whisky. Her little girls cut and drew
maps and pademelons. The widow
groaned and watched the candle.
And the old man lay in the cold back room.

On the third day, friends arrived with the box.
A locum agreed to sign the second piece of paper.
The mother drove to the city and bought two fish.
Chunks of firewood were chopped and stacked.
In the night, a corona was thrown around the moon.
Frost glittered on the bracken fern like longing.
And the old man lay in the cold back room.

On the fourth day, people drove up the mountain
and down the valley to see the old man
and comfort the widow. The maid and the mother
laid food on the table. Songs were sung. Dung
was burnt. The fish were eaten, the box painted.
A banker signed the third piece of paper.
And the old man lay in the cold back room.

On the fifth day, we raised the old man into
the box. We carried the box to the truck, past weeping
men and raven punk women. We drove two hours
to the furnace. The widow sobbed and walked away.
The old man lay in the furnace as we drove back
up the mountain and down the valley.
We made chowder from the bones of the fish.

Coquun evening

Give up smoking, they keep saying, but have you ever
spent a turning summer evening on the shores
of *Coquun* as blue and orange flirt and tumble
on the harbour and the dying world flings out
glory in defiance, so you take a drag
on a cigarette and poison burns your gorge and
you are momentarily a sheet-bend love-knot
of pleasure and anguish? The pilot boat planes past
fetching a bulk carrier. Terns reel and
vie for roosts on their starboard mark. Behind you
mauve mounds of cumulus are heaping in the north.
All of it. All of it! Exquisite and flawed, it draws
from you an exhalation of praise that is as brief
as evening hues, as light as the land breeze.

Hazing the geese

We bide on the edge
of our shallow listless lake,
cloaked in topaz.
We guard our grievous creation.
Air-touched mine-spoil steeps
acid from clods and burdens
the water with metals.
We stare in the glass
waiting for the geese.
Hosts of fish rise up
and float to shore.

They come. A spear of geese
sweeps over us with steady
wing-beat tattoo.
We ready ourselves.
They have each other—
fly tight as garlic cloves.
They have the sky—
our necks are sore with gazing.
Muscular backs hold straight
their tapering arrow-heads
circling the lake
scanning for rest.

We wail in primal warning.
We bark. We flap and squawk.
We're jealous fowl
on perilous roosts.
We cry in pity's name

we weep with envy
and shame to spare them
lighting on our dead lake
and scalding their guts.

Leachate luxury beckons,
honeyed poison draws
and down they come
in beautiful clamour
to join our ruin.

Meeting Ezra in the Museum

I sit opposite Ezra
stirring my tea, thinking
about sand-whipped shrubs.
Behind his ear our past
hangs like honeysuckle.
He must detect the scent.

I vibrate against
the décor. I want Ezra
to tell me what he thinks.
He holds my poem crisp,
reading. I trace the serif
lizard tracks.

You are a poem, but
your poem's naught—
A smear of it is on his chin.

He has set a lure
bobbing on my wave.
If I swallow it,
a hard clear filament
will catch my mouth
in his hands.

My wrist brushes my breast
as I bring my hand to my cheek.
Its plumpness soothes me.

But Dryad, this is poetry!—

Men smother ripe melons
with straw then pity
their tender skins.
Men baffle coastal shrubs
with windy gaze, so we
grow low and stiff.

Then they accuse:
you take your ideas
from the men you sleep with.

His pencil moves.
A trellis, a pair
of secateurs.

He signs my appellation:
"H.D. *Imagiste*."

Up I spring,
like a tendril
of wild violet.

[Notes]

"You are a poem, but your poem's naught" reportedly said by Ezra Pound to HD
    in the British Museum tea room in 1912, according to her account of it in *End to*
    Torment (H.D *End to Torment* p12). He is also reportedly signed off the poem for
    her "H.D. *Imagiste*."
This phrase, "You are a poem, though your poem's naught," appears in Robert
    Browning's 'Transcendence' a poem Ezra Pound enjoyed, and in HD's Asphodel
    and HERmione, citing Browning.
Ripe melons smothered in straw is an image drawn from H.D's poem 'Sheltered
    Garden' appearing in *Collected Poems* 1912-1944.
"But Dryad, this is poetry!" Attributed to Ezra Pound by H.D in *End to Torment.* p18.

Holding a long-dead fish

This fossil fish, in hieroglyph,
presents his eons-long koan
of natural selection.

Embody, little fish, the paradox
of art and accident! *Luck* is
the mother of invention.

Your bones and alimentary
tract are the stony residue
of serendipity and

dodged fatalities. Or were you
among the luckless fish
with terminal mutations?

Petrified forever, you wink
and stir our old fears
of teleology. Could this

elaborate life be a mere
by-product of aimless chemistry?
Unthinkable!

Dream of the seafarer

He sails alone over the sunken city.
His keel is fleet above dead eaves and canopy.
The upwelling river-grave delivers
garlands of sea grasses from the past
as his shadow cruises over slime-wrapped suburbs,
now the range-ways of the scale-herd.

For what crime is he exiled?
Self-loathing, and a bearing like a cyclone, unclothed
and hurling wild the weakened weed shreds.
But uncautious creatures come to him.
Petrels will spend many miles at air and then
find rest with him on deck,
hove-to aloft the dolphin-dunes.

Rain-hives are striding wide across the fly-way,
mustering for an uproar. Strobing lightning
sets afire his wish to hazard all his holdings.
Deep, deep, many leagues, lies the sin of his
bereavement and retreat. He beats above,
storm jib taut, seeking out the wind-lift...

Early morning at the river

Mist lifts as the river's skin
unwinds under the sun's touch.
Likewise, whiffs of self will rise
on cyan days when light glances
wavelets, leafs and faces.
What you love will answer you in kind.

To be coaxed in fondness, to be drawn
by sense, it is no lessening. River haze is
fluvial reach to fondle in turn the ferns
while my own hand kneads water
and my fog curls and disperses,
dowsing my beloveds.

Felix silvestris

on the occasion of my sister turning forty.

Let's get something straight:
the primness I'm putting out is a put on.
My paws placed together and the pout
I perfected where I learned preening—
in slick-tiled Egyptian bath-houses: it's all show.
Smooth-chested dusky sons of river-traders
taught me this: you don't get cream
without a little theatre.

It takes a big effort, this effortless poise:
little habits of style refined over millennia.

Ever since I walked alone into your cave
in the Fertile Crescent, I've been toying
with civilisation like a bell-ball,
a la jaguar. Untameable? Maybe, but cool
in a catastrophe and a warm patch of sun
is enough to slow the temper.

Bastet protects the household, bringer
of joy and love. If you're feeling chilled
it's kinda gonna be coz you ain't been invited
to the centrally-heated lounge of my affection,
where the love ointment flows,
sans affection.
                    But you who have felt
that rough damp scrape of a tongue,
heard the husky roll of my love, well,
you won't have any questions.

Persephone

She wants me to return, I know.
When I'm gone, she skews my tale:
rubs it so I gleam,
makes my love a horror.
Snatched away! (they say) while skipping
'mid the daisies on the surface.
Imprisoned! (they cry) below the ground
in hot fathoms that she has not seen.
Well, I have seen them.
I ate their chthonic fruits willingly
for love, for candour.

The Host of Many taught me
egalitarianism, iconoclasm,
and the magic of circles.
In seven days he showed me
lights that can't be seen but in darkness:
labours only fruitful after pain,
how to thresh corn and welcome death,
to bury seeds and bring forth sprouts.

My mind swelled like a pomegranate,
ruddy and firm.

I was restive on the surface,
arranged among artful flowers,
tastefully cloaking the soil.
Why don't my visits satisfy?
Would she have eternal springtime?
Birth without death? She's preposterous.

And yet I know she cannot bear
to hear my other names spoken,
or the scent of spirit
as votaries carry me down
murmuring rot and sod,
and I catechise each one.

Voices from the swamp's edge

You want us trapped in stalks and shivering
your breathy tunes just as you dreamed we'd be
your dream composed from our captivity:
but now we speak.
Our roses were not false but they became
imagined in the dark while our old enemy the night
heaped up around us. Your misgiving branched
and grew gnarled into complaint,
made excuses for the trunk, that wood, your triumph.
Are the women that you sing about made by your song?

No.

Your eyes are springs: illusion pours on us
and we are short of breath from cold while
your song sings of warm and breezy sighs
upon your fleece. No!

Under muzzy morning as the sun rose
we fought. You heard just the ditty on your flute.
It is the source of your art, your genius,
and our ruin. After your lies, you think
you will regain heaven with Art?
And we your silent muses?

No.

We are on the swamp's edge now.
While you gloated over dawn's envy
and your conceit rampaged alone, we

escaped and made ourselves into reeds.
We swayed together. A chorus of birds hid
the susurrus of our breath and the wind
drew voice from us. They're not sweet nothings,
the whispered rumours of your hated kiss.
Though we have no evidence, the mark
of our bite on your chest attests.

Windy music shivers from the reed bed.
You close your eyes and listen to your own
sonorous, vain, monotonous note
blowing on the hollows of your hand.

[Notes]

This poem is adapted from parts of Mallarmé's 'L'après-midi d'un faune' and
   Ovid's tale of Pan pursuing the chaste nymph Syrinx, who hides from him and is
   transformed into reeds which he then plucks and uses as his famous pipe.

The fires

Darkness rolls and hurls fistfuls of cinders
on the wind with news from the front.
Fluttering ash-flakes fall like leaflets dropped
from enemy planes before the razing, warning:
there will be hours and years of retreat.

Flying foxes tumble from the sky
as flames suck breath from their lungs.
The road is melting.
Maddened 'roos scramble for the gully.
The weeping Premier promises on the telly,

      help is coming,

keep your babies floating in the dam
as the coal black fury leaps the ridge.
Wet towels shield your heads and their short breaths
poignant with trust. You tell them:

You're not going to die while you're little.

It's too much.

Your arms and legs are ingots longing
for the earth and its solid iron core.
Around you – *thud   thud* – parrots
drop dead into the flames in relief.
There's no need to beat their wings
and frantically search for water
or shelter or a political solution
any longer.

In the silence twelve hours later
two sobbing fireys vomit together
in a wrecked forest,
so still and dry
it crumbles
at the touch.

[Notes]

"How are we going to keep two babies afloat in a dam?" Daniele Marshall.
  Quoted in 'Bushfire survivors tell of lucky escapes.' A.M. February 2009.
  http://www.abc.net.au/am/content/2008/s2485770.htm
"You're not going to die while you're little." Helen Goudy. Qtd in 'Victorian
  bushfires: Chintin mother shelters with children in neighbour's dam.' ABC News.
  February 2014. http://www.abc.net.au/news/2014-02-10/victoria-fires-chintin-
  mother-shelters-children-in-dam/5250208

Inside the eel

Down on the Co-op wharves an
Italian restaurateur bought
a five-foot eel, asked for a knife
and gutted it on the aging planks.

Fat pearlescent pouches of organ
spilled from a cavity painted
sky-blue aquamarine.
He tossed them to the gulls.

On the deck, Paul has now
dismantled a winch and cleaned
its neat cogs and pawls with kero.
These guts yoke gales.

I have no word for *saṃsāra*.
I want to take wing
and catch the innards,
or put my head
into the wind's mouth.

Orison

At the dissolution, when all our sieges,
laid in fervour, crumble away defeated,
lie quietly here with me in the forest,
ashy-soled sister.

Swags are rolled out under the greying red gums'
dry and darkling canopy. Hushed and starry,
deeper into hours without sleep, tonight I'm
offering you my

eager heart unguardedly. Will you hear this
praise in clumsy orison, peerless sister?
Meet me in your mightiest aspect: never
consort or helpmeet.

Dawn in the cremation ground. You are rising
with the sliding darklessness. Left behind, I'm
mapless and I search the burning
earth for you, my friend.

Rites of the freedwoman

I think the Romans understood free love.
How a woman in her middle age collects
myrtle, mint, and common wine
for libations at the beach.

She should also offer rushes
so I do not hesitate.
I follow you down
rocks and jump into the sea.

Venus Libertina's cave is
carved by waves into the cliff.
Open to the aqua swell and you
disappear inside it.
Which of us presides here?
Who comes for instruction?

I am on the sand and in
the blue above an eagle coasts.
Ancient pagans knew the holy
is not locked in marriage or
sacristies. Affection flows
divine through each encounter.

Into this pink-stoned pool
we immerse like pilgrims.
We will have no hearth but body.
We will swear no oath, but cries
of praise will escape from us like
startled fish erupting from the shallows.

Smashing it all to pieces and bringing it all back

Aquila audux folds its umber wings with
regal eye on me in offering.
I kneel in trembling thanks and take
the power to dismantle engineering.

Wing-whoosh reefs up concrete from the creeks.
Talons grip the bark of fallen stags and
hurl them over drains to curb the water.
Blade of my beak tears the weeds away.
Cry from my throat summonses cedar saplings
in the streets. Decades are pouring from me,
raising trees. I flex cellulose
against the steel, and steel retreats.

Hunting over roads, my glower tears
asphalt and I roll the chunks aloft
between my thighs and shed waste to the soil.
I work the sticky balls down to pitch
marbles that drop harmless to the ground.

Water-fowl fluster at my passing shadow,
squall and shriek in circles as I dive.
Concrete cracks and shatters. I'm the eye of
bird-whorl as the flooding reed beds rise and
water claims back the wading lands.

In my wake, the flocks return and settle.

Crowds of people stare in awe but soon
grow quarrelsome. My mantle-tearing slows them
down and bows them round, meandering.

Elders and kids, I hope, will be delighted
at the birds' return. As for the rest,
they may carp, but none would ever
choose to put it back.

Coronach with grey butcherbird

who?   *we?*

He throws melodious appeals.
The light slants and I
bend towards it
seeking counsel.

heat   heat   more

weep
        weep-in-here.

His knell grants leave to cry.
The warm comes on, on.
He keens for temperate cool
and I moan back,
for earth and all our error.

well-and-good, he soothes,

throw   throw
do-it.

Lament is day:
it ends
        and it returns.

after drought comes charity:
all the clouds will burst,
and rain will gather, days on days,
our motes of song to earth.

Beside the eel

Here where
the bronze lithe creek
hides an
eel still
in the shallows,

time undulates, and
the creature
with it
sinuates
into shadow.
Umber under umbra.

Light lights
on the creek
face and parts:
some
leaps up,
shows me the canopy.
Some
slants down,
shows me eel on rock
and I
exalt
this mystery.

I am receiving light.
I take it in.
I cast it back.
Reach,

in desire,
stroking rock
and muscle.
It riffles
on leaves
that riffle
on me.

Sky surface substrate
all at once.

Making shelter

You will walk bare foot in a wind-made place
beside the salty grass, shouting sea and beaten shrubs.
Yield or be twisted: these are your options.

You had better pause and pull yourself together.
This wind is going to outlast your morning.
It will outlast your youth and your life.
To stand against it is to fall or sweep away,
as she-oaks have fallen,
as cabbage moths are swept.

You had better take a fist of earth to hold.
As your bark arms flex
you will flower and make shelter
for herbs. Be patient:
there will come a time when your steadiness
has gathered so much life around it,
you are a dune,
with fresh water pooling at your feet.

After life

In Terry's shed
in Tomago
he's got
a loo,
a bucket,
a kitchenette
and a furnace,
door ajar
with
a flaming skeleton
inside.

Metal limbs
and joints
survive the fire
and are tipped
into the bucket.
On a tray,
skull bits,
bone shards
and an enamel
name plate: 'Nola.'
"No man,
nor woman
neither,"
(I thought).

Terry's blades
wear down,
grinding

the bone
to powder.

In four days
he'll give you
your jar of dust;
for disposal
or safe keeping.

The floods

Flooding, vomiting over walls,
hurling down fences.
After years of sandbagging,
after years of siege, we dream we're rushing
over banks, drowning forms, queues and categories.
We are carrying the day at last,
buoyant and inexorable.

Flooding, smothering roads and walls.
Hillslopes yield to current and collapse.
Soils and trees join the tepid gravy
urging unrelenting past the door,
oozing loose our heavy luxury
into a mass of rubbish.

Snakes and bandits turn up with the water;
Wild teens dare each other to leap in;
Nurses follow in the ebb searching
for torn seeds in the brown whorls—
All of us are strangers now
with no water we can drink.

One day, one day, wet will cease receding.
We will pour out and reclaim.
In my dream, this is the day.
In my dream, we burst like clouds to flood
the mines and catch the deluge.

Here we come, we overtop the sky.
I dream we are droplets pouring down.

Cascading as one, we thunder on the roofs
of bankers and mining bosses.
Friends, we're drenched,
we cannot hold.
We will spill, we will spill.

Going wrong

To be mistaken brings good fortune.

I am walking in a dying forest
under needles falling
from a stately mountain oak.

Many dry and stressful
years he has withstood
to come to this—
parching and defeated
in a birdless copse.

I make fruitless
troth to him:
I love you.
No other creature
stirs or cries.

Many times you told me
speech is bootless:
what you needed
to survive was rain.
I don't have the means
to call it in.
I can't
undo this wrong.
So the greenwood dies
with love in surfeit.

Even now,
I throw my spirit out
to its thinning crown
and cry
again
— *I love!* —
as if those words
could guard against the drying.
As if amends to you were possible.

Ocean mistress

Here we take beyond in and
reach with mind uncut,
so that light, wave and tern
are self.

It is for this we risk
humiliation and drowning:
to be seized and
to be free.
We swim to yield
to that blue and yet
resist.

It would carry us to
depths we cannot pilot.
We brawl back to the shallows
where flood tide plies waves
and the torsional swell
is a many-armed love
wooing, "Come! Come!"

At that call,
an urgent anti-
self springs
into the current,
is borne out to far
pods and shoals.

Eurydice and the lyrebird

She flows, expelled, downslope into the forest.
She is excess, she is run-off. Mighty
as it is, water has no path but down.
Its power, never willed, cannot refuse
a gradient. Ancient earth-mass
lugs her and she courses to that urge—
withholding her unruly accusation: (*faithless!*)
She carries it instead, in woman runnels
leaking to the soil, puddling to a soak
dark below the canopy.

On the bright bank above,
his silhouette fleets. She hears
the rapid liquid airs of many birds,
out of reach and growing faint.

Sapling asana

i.

The brush is plumb.

Plants haul themselves up light-wire.
Up into cockatoo space, ambition space.
Up into the ways of winds and big wings,
broken boughs and squabbling.

Below, bass wire plays an earthways fall.
Damp leaves furrow sombre.
Turkeys forage, eyes on mulch.
Their way cluttered with windfall.

Mountain tension lengthens
like a dancer and falls clod by clod.
Forest giants fell here.
Sinewy neck-thick vines self-tangle in coils
where light poured on the floor.

ii.

Hold still while you
discern the fount.

Wave slowly and clasp
a stripling giant.

Hitch to the canopy, quick,
before your weight becomes too great
and the whole lot tumbles down.

Visiting the island, 1839

Elizabeth Gould stalks a Newcastle parlour
like a watchful egret. The room looks north
and takes her with its gaze to the wild estuary.
Spoonbills rise and wheel and she wants
to plunge her face into that place.

At dawn she embarks with the baby.
Mangroves gild and Franklin's fat hand
beats the gunwales. A kingfisher escorts them
from despoilment, trilling the swan's song
of Ash Island's rainforest.

Their tent is pitched in a clearing ringed
by cedar and ash and hung with strangle-vine.
She herself fell into the branches of
an ornithologist and grew down
his torso to this blooming island,
pre-lapsarian glory.

A storm arrives with evening.
Lightning spotlights fruit bats reeling.
In the morning, Franklin suckles
like an artwork. John warms tea
on the camp stove.

Ash Island is slick with rain, ready
to be sketched.

Song of Scorn

Many buried cicadas crawl out
decades later from the earth, summoned
by sorrow's sudden shower.

Remorse is pulsing through an afternoon:
rasp, rasp though the scorch-light.
Blood rhythm rises to it.

There will be misfortune that is not
fixed by labour, program or device.
It will simply be borne.

It clambers from the soil.
It neither needs nor knows you.
All your songs will be wanting.

I shudder with an urge to throw the window
open to the heat and let the panting
fruit bats in to drink the bath.

I can give them melon in my poem.
I'm not impotent or fast behind
the walls: I'm hospitable

as a nomad. I'm a cool sandstone
cave and all my pools belong to Earth.
Darkling now, her cooling clay plinks.

Bats are bumbling out again into
the garden, lapping flower nectar,
screeching wonder at survival.

She is turning. I can feel a tectonic
flexing of her arm against us.
Storms like these will be retold

for another thousand years by poor
and bare forked animals like us.
She will make the towers

all a desolation. Your works will live in
songs of scorn and we will be
cursed by our descendants.

Three forests

Paddy's Brush

Paddy's Brush lies beyond a short wooden bridge
where three people lay down in the snow
in 1995, blockading Stewart's Brook long enough
for the law and clemency to save it.

There is no track to follow, just grassy ground
under silver stringys, languid in the wind,
casually hiding a dark green streak
of Antarctic beech, cleft into the plateau.

The beech clutch their ground with hard knuckles.
They bunch and branch, darkly sufficient.
The cold air is clotted by a hidden
lyrebird belting out Gondwana medleys.

Sit still there long enough to be forgotten.
Catch sight of your irrelevance like
log-runners turning up in the gloom.

Leard Forest

I'm tramping lightless through the night towards
the glow of industry, hours ahead, in Leard Forest.
My gratitude billows breathy vapour on
Scott's back as he leads us there in silence.

It's easy walking in the grassy box-gum past the smudged
white trunks adorned with hidden *Microchiroptera*.

There may be yellow-bellied sheathtails
huddled snout-down in any of these branches.

Sweet rarity of hidden bats.
They need only tiny hollows,
smaller than the ball of my fist
at dawn as the clearing opens.

The heart is an animal. It yowls,
confused at how it came to be caged
and pacing, useless, side to side.

Chunky limbs and sides of white box
lie in broken windrows
pushed across the clearing.

When the rain comes,
there is no canopy to shield
my drenched and shivering vanity.

Any heart so exposed might swap
bravado for caution, and hide
in the bushes from workmen.

Upper Fallbrook

At the Jump Creek confluence
forest oaks are burdened with the rain.

Decay is the process: lily and moss ruins
are picked over by scrub wrens and shat out.

Rust and lichen bloom. All our works corrode.
All our hours of striving tumble back.

In the Glennies upper catchment,
an idea was dug into the soil.

In 1989, Barrie in court, Marg before the dozer,
stopped the road from cutting through Mount Royal.

He said, "I'll build a house, and it will last
for twenty years. It will be all I need."

A king in a fairy tale,
makes such contracts with dark agents

but humus squats in all your castles.
(Bottom-up sog! No masters!)

Ideas unfurl and rot hourly
as fungi on abandoned logs.

Mushroom man, there are no borders.
An epiphyte-cloaked bulloak's longing

for light will at last give way
to its massive fealty to sod.

Twenty years went and humus came
to mulch your piles of old reports

and points of claim. The flooding
brook swept down your barrages.

Urge,   urge,   urge.
Living presses waste
between its parts
to the last sigh;
that is its nature.
Fuel will be consumed,
is all the law.

Dear friend, old men have told me
the rub of silver against the world
makes it shine— "the coin in use
means business."

the paper fruiting through
the courts' triumphal florets,
makes safe the forest,
then falls and rots into the soil.

Stillness is death:
death is not stillness.
We fall, we fall,
and the humus opens
loving arms.

[Notes]

"the coin in use means business" – David Malouf, 'Two Odes of Horace' Earth
  Hour. University of Queensland Press. 2014.

A blessing

How shall we gather
what griefs destroy?

Justice Kirby, receiving honours,
spoke to the scholars of love—

greater than pride and wealth,
enduring beyond vanities.

Soil fungi love-process their nitrogen;
foliage throws open its arms
to photons; phytoplankton love-breathe
carbon, cycle it through
the turquoise homelands
in squid bellies.

Splendour.
Splendour.

With what shall we carry?
With what shall we mend?

[Notes]

"How shall we gather what griefs destroy" William Blake, from 'The School Boy'
"Love transcends even scholarship, cleverness and university degrees. It is greater
than pride and wealth. It endures when worldly vanities fade." The Hon. Justice
Michael Kirby, 'But the greatest of these is love: Address on the conferral of the
honourary degree of doctor of Griffith University,' December 2008.

Acknowledgments

'Open the window and let her fly out,' published in *Women of Words 2016-2018*, Ed. Jeanette Hoppe, 2020. 'Sand whiting,' published in *Cordite* No Theme IV, 2019; 'Fluid dynamics,' published in *Rabbit 26: Belonging*, October 2018; 'Smashing it all to piece and bringing it all back,' published in *Plumwood Mountain* Volume 5 Number 2, August 2018; 'After Life,' published in *Visible Ink 29: The End*, 2017; 'Water Song,' published in *The Dangar Island Garbage Boat: Newcastle Poetry Prize Anthology 2016*; 'Rites of Passage,' published in *Presume a Flat Horizon: Newcastle Poetry at the Pub Anthology 2016*; earlier version of 'Futility (Leard forest, winter 2014)' published in *The Disappearing*, Red Room Company, 2016; 'Paradise Losing,' published in *Overland* 220, Spring 2015; "Felix Silvestris," published in *Newcastle Poetry at the Pub Anthology 2015*.

www.ingramcontent.com/pod-product-compliance
Lightning Source LLC
Chambersburg PA
CBHW031007090426
42737CB00008B/712